uick
&
easy

Green
Anole Care

Quick & Easy Green Anole Care

Project Team
Editor: Tom Mazorlig
Copy Editor: Carl Schutt
Design: Patricia Escabi
Series Design: Mary Ann Kahn

T.F.H. Publications
President/CEO: Glen S. Axelrod
Executive Vice President: Mark E. Johnson
Publisher: Christopher T. Reggio
Production Manager: Kathy Bontz

T.F.H. Publications, Inc.
One TFH Plaza
Third and Union Avenues
Neptune City, NJ 07753

Library of Congress Cataloging-in-Publication Data
Hunziker, Raymond E.
Quick and easy green anole care / Ray Hunziker.
p. cm.
Includes index.
ISBN 0-7938-1021-3 (alk. paper)
    1.   Green anoles as pets. I. Title.
SF459.L5H86 2005
639.3'9548—dc22
2005004683

This book has been published with the intent to provide accurate and authoritative information in regard to the subject matter within. While every precaution has been taken in preparation of this book, the author and publisher expressly disclaim responsibility for any errors, omissions, or adverse effects arising from the use or application of the information contained herein. The techniques and suggestions are used at the reader's discretion and are not to be considered a substitute for veterinary care. If you suspect a medical problem, consult your veterinarian.

The Leader in Responsible Animal Care for over 50 years!™
www.tfhpublications.com

Table of Contents

Introducing the
Green Anole

I f you are reading this book, chances are you already have purchased a charming little green anole from your local pet store and now want to know how to take care of him. While these lizards are relatively hardy, they do have specific needs that you must meet if your new pet is going to survive. If you already have an anole, you should probably skip ahead to the housing and feeding chapters so you can make sure your anole has a proper environment as soon as possible. Be sure to read the rest of the book later, as it will provide you with a lot of interesting and useful information about your colorful critters.

It is best if you read this book *before* you purchase a green anole. Reading the book first will allow you learn what exactly is involved in the care of one and to help you decide if you will be willing to provide that care for the full life of your anole. Also, you will be able to have a comfortable home all set up and waiting for your anole, which will ease his transition into his new life with you.

What Is an Anole?

First things first: Anoles are reptiles, with scaly skin and fully shelled eggs that distinguish them from the amphibians. Reptiles are

Green anoles are small, climbing lizards commonly found throughout the southeastern United States.

usually called "cold-blooded," but that's really not a fair label. They just have a different approach to heating their bodies than do "warm-blooded" critters like you and me. Specifically, anoles belong to the group of reptiles called lizards. There are more that 300 species of anoles, although only a few can be found in pet stores.

Any food an animal eats produces energy. This energy can be used for lots of things—growth, movement, reproduction, and more. The warm-blooded animals use much of their energy to keep the body warm. They are able to maintain a high level of activity this way, but they have less energy to devote to the other activities mentioned above. Reptiles warm the body by basking in the sun and don't "waste" their food energy to do it. When fully warmed by the sun, most reptiles have a body temperature pretty close to that of a mammal. When reptiles get too cool (at night or during the winter), they become less active or even dormant. Because of this frugal use of energy, a reptile needs far less food than a mammal or bird of the same size, so looking down on the "primitive, cold-blooded" reptiles is a disservice. From a certain point of view, they're more efficient than we are. It's also worth knowing that different species of reptiles have adapted to be comfortable and active at different temperatures, depending on their habitat.

Anoles as a group are fairly small lizards, ranging from 4 to 20 inches. In most species, half to two-thirds of their total length is the tail. Anoles are mostly arboreal (tree climbers), and they need that tail for balance. Some species are more ground dwelling (terrestrial). Most species of anoles eat insects and other invertebrates (such as spiders and worms). A few species are big enough to eat small frogs, baby birds, other lizards, and small mammals. All of the anoles come from the tropical and subtropical areas of the western hemisphere in a range of different habitats. However, most are found in forests.

The toes of an anole are specialized for climbing. An anole can run up a vertical tree trunk, hang upside down on a leaf—or even climb glass—all because of his amazing toes. However, the toes do not have suction cups. The tips are flattened and have tiny ridges on the bottoms, and these ridges are marvelous. If you highly magnify the toe ridges, such as under an electron microscope, you will find that they are covered with tiny hooks. Glass, smooth as it looks, is not smooth at all—under magnification, it has thousands of tiny projections. The hooks on an anole's toe ridges catch on the tiny, unseen projections on glass or any other smooth surface. An anole is like a tiny mountain climber, putting hooks into crevices and hanging on.

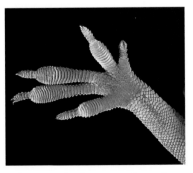

The toe pads of green anoles and other species allow them to cling to virtually any surface—including glass.

Introducing the Green Anole   7

Anoles have other interesting features of their anatomy and behavior. One is the throat fan, more correctly called a dewlap. Attached to the throat is a stiff rib of cartilage that the anole can flare outward. When the cartilage is erect, it stretches the skin of the throat into a flat half circle. The throat fan makes the anole's head look much bigger; it is also vividly colored, usually bright pink in green anoles, but often red or orange in other species. Almost all anole species have throat fans, and they are usually much more developed in the males, who use the fan-flaring display to intimidate other males. This way, a strong male can claim a territory and the opportunity to mate with local females.

Another curious anatomical feature of anoles, which they share with many other lizards and snakes, is the pineal eye. There is an enlarged scale on the top of the head that actually covers a rudimentary third eye. It does not form an image, but it can sense light and darkness. It is a built-in timer that sets the lizards' biological clocks. When it senses that days are growing shorter, it signals to the lizard that it is time to hibernate. When it senses the days are growing longer, added to the stimulus of higher temperatures, it triggers the enlarge-

Herp Is the Word

Throughout this book, you will see the term *herps*. This word refers to both reptiles and amphibians together. *Herps* comes from the word *herpetology*, which is the study of reptiles and amphibians. When speaking about the hobby of keeping reptiles and amphibians, you can call it the *herp hobby*. *Herpetoculture* is the keeping and breeding of reptiles and amphibians. A *herper* is someone who participates in the herp hobby or herpetoculture (also called a *herp hobbyist*).

These terms are handy to know, not just for reading this book, but because you will see them in other herp publications and the Internet, and hear other herp hobbyists use these words.

Quick & Easy Green Anole Care

Male anoles have an expandable pouch (dewlap) beneath their lower jaws. They erect the dewlap during territorial displays.

ment of the sex organs and the beginning of breeding activity. It also tells an anole when he needs get into or out of the sun.

The Green Anole

The focus of this book is on one species of anole—the green anole—the most popular species in the American pet trade. Green anoles inhabit much of the southeastern United States, from extreme southeastern Virginia to the Florida Keys and westward to southern Texas. There are introduced populations on a few Caribbean islands, Oahu, and northeastern Mexico, but almost all the green anoles in the world are found within U.S. borders.

Green anoles feed on small arthropods—insects and spiders, mostly. They spend a large percentage of their waking hours hunting, or at least alert to strike at any unwary bug that wanders close enough. The snout is long and relatively flattened, with large teeth (compared to his tiny size) in each jaw. Anoles hunt visually, looking for any small, moving creature. They focus carefully with the movable eyes and then lunge forward, snapping the prey in their jaws. Some anoles are quite good at catching flying insects such as butterflies, moths, flies, and even dragonflies, all of which are quickly crunched and swallowed.

American "Chameleons"

The green anole was once called the "American chameleon" in pet shops. It is *not* a chameleon. Chameleons are strange Old World (meaning the eastern hemisphere; the western hemisphere is the New World) lizards with opposable toes, prehensile tails, and independently moving eyes. Chameleons definitely aren't that closely related to anoles, and they are much more difficult to care for than anoles.

Why did they ever call the green anole a "chameleon?" The answer is simple—because chameleons can change color, and so can green anoles. It is not because they are related. In fact, many reptiles and amphibians can change color to some degree. Chameleons can change to many colors and patterns; green anoles are limited to greens and browns and can't make any patterns, although some can get small spots. The throat and belly are always white. The color change is not instantaneous, but it is fast. An anole can turn from brown to green, or vice versa, in about a minute.

In chameleons and green anoles, the color changing ability is not used mostly for camouflage, contrary to popular belief. Actually, the color has more to do with mood and temperature. Anoles are brown when they are sleeping or cold, and they turn bright green when they are warmed up and active. Also, an active, warm male anole will turn brown again when he confronts an intruder (i.e., another male anole) in his territory. A sick anole will be brown, but he will be a darker brown than a sleeping/cold anole, and he will not change to green when he warms up.

Territoriality

Anoles are generally territorial animals, and the green anole is no

Scientific Names

You may have noticed that sometimes there are strange looking words in italics that appear after the name of an animal. This is the scientific name, and each animal only has one scientific name. Biologists determine the scientific name of each animal based on what other animals it is related to. The first part of the name is called the *genus*; the second part is the *species*. This combination of genus and species is unique for each animal.

The reason we have scientific names is so that scientists all over the world can talk about each animal without worrying about language barriers or other similar animals being confused with the one they want to discuss. Several anoles species are predominantly green, but only the North American green anole is called *Anolis carolinensis*.

If you use the genus name once, you can abbreviate it to the first letter when you write about it later. So, if I was talking about green anoles again, I could just type *A. carolinensis*. Also, if I wanted to talk about all the lizards in the same genus as the green anole, I would just say *Anolis*.

Scientific names may be confusing and hard to pronounce at first, but they actually do make things easier. If you decide to do more reading about keeping pet reptiles and amphibians, you should become accustomed to scientific names, since hobbyist use them frequently.

exception. Their territorial behavior is fascinating and fun to watch and so complex that many scientific papers have been written on the subject. We have space to mention only the basics here.

The male is the more territorial of the sexes, but larger females will often dominate smaller ones. The size of an anole's territory is variable, depending on the terrain and the number of anoles in the area. In most cases, a green anole claims an area several feet in diameter.

Green anoles actually range in color from green to brown and can change color between those two extremes.

When an intruder enters the territory, the resident male moves perpendicular to him and flares his dewlap. In green anoles, the throat fan varies from greenish white (not common) to bright pink (most common) to almost red. The brighter the fan, the stronger and more dominant the animal. The intruder may return the fan-flaring display. In addition to erecting the throat fan, either or both males may do a "head bob," jerking the head up and down rapidly, or "push-ups," in which the whole front of the body is jerked up and down. Usually the interloper will take the hint at this point and back off. If not, the resident male will lunge at him and chase him around until he leaves the area. The interaction is mostly display and bluff without actual violence occurring. Occasionally the combatants will get close enough to bite at each other. Rarely, the resident male will lose the battle and be run off by a larger and more dominant intruder, who will then take over his territory.

Although green anoles climb extremely well, they usually are not seen high up in trees. Rather, they seem to prefer shrubbery, walls, fences, and small trees. They are rarely seen above 15 feet or so, and they are also rarely seen on the ground. They prefer to jump from bush to bush, and they are incredibly acrobatic. Anoles can jump quite far for their size.

All in all, the green anole is a marvelously adapted little lizard and, as we shall soon see, makes a fine pet.

Pets for Kids?

Green anoles are often sold as good pets for children and people who have never had lizards before. While they are inexpensive, interesting, and hardy little lizards, their care is actually more involved than most children or fist-time lizard owners are prepared to offer. Most of this care is not too difficult to provide, but it does involve learning about proper lighting and heating and providing a nutritious diet of live insects. If you read this book before you buy an anole and decide that caring for one is more complicated or time-consuming than you would like, there are a number of other lizards that might be better choices for you, such as leopard geckos, fat-tailed geckos, or blue-tongued skinks.

The major problem with anoles as pets for children is handling. Kids like to touch and hold their pets. Being tiny, fast, and rather

Different anole species have differently colored dewlaps. The orange dewlap here belongs to a Bahaman brown anole.

Physical fights between territorial male anoles are rare, but they do happen. Usually, after a series bluffs and displays, one runs off before an actual fight occurs.

high-strung, anoles do not take well to handling. Additionally, their tails will come off if they are pulled or grabbed, a likely event when being held by a young child. They are best thought of as interesting display animals. If you want to get a lizard your child can handle, consider a bearded dragon, a spiny-tailed agama (also called uromastyx), a leopard gecko, or a blue-tongued skink.

Anoles are interesting and beautiful display animals. They will thrive in a naturalistic terrarium with live plants and possibly some other small animals (more on that in later chapters). In such a setting, they offer a small window into nature right in your living room. They can teach children to respect life and nature and to consider the small and odd animals to be as important as the large and cute ones.

Getting the Best Anole

Most of you will not be collecting your own anoles. So, when you're standing in the pet shop and looking at a cage filled with anoles, how do you choose a healthy one? Selecting a healthy anole is at least half the battle in keeping one successfully.

Be suspicious of anoles kept in crowded cages. The stress of constantly battling for food, water, and territory can take its toll. Also, be wary of anoles kept in cages without adequate heat and lighting. Look at the cage substrate—a dirty cage is the number one sign of lackluster care on the part of the keeper.

When selecting an anole, it is helpful to look at the base of the tail. If he is skinny with protruding hips, like this one, it is best to consider a different individual.

Look for an anole that is alert. He should look at you as you approach the cage. He may even jump around and attempt to hide. Anoles have excellent eyesight and are always interested in what is going on around them, even outside the cage, so one that does not acknowledge your presence may be ill.

Look at color. Healthy anoles who are being kept at the right temperature are bright green during their waking hours. Don't ever buy a mottled, dark brown anole. These poor creatures are really on their way out.

One of the best overall indications of an anole's health is his eyes. The eyes should bulge slightly from their sockets. If they are sunken in it means the animal is dehydrated, which usually happens when an anole gets too weak to eat or drink. An anole with sunken eyes is often on death's doorstep.

Anoles that are malnourished begin to show it quickly in the pelvic girdle (hip region) and tail. Well-fed anoles show only the faintest outlines of their bones, but a starving anole will have the lines of the pelvic bones clearly visible beneath the skin. The tail develops a kinked appearance as the muscles atrophy and the skin hugs close to the vertebrae. Even the vertebrae along the top of the back and at the base

Quick & Easy Green Anole Care

of the skull may be apparent. The ribs stick out to a grotesque degree. I think you get the idea—a starving anole is really just skin and bones, because all of the fat and most of the muscles have been consumed.

Finally, confirm the sex of the anole, especially if you're buying more than one. Remember, males have large postanal pores (just behind the vent) that are absent in females. Males are also a bit larger than females and have slightly larger heads in proportion to body size. Although both sexes technically have throat fans, those of males are distinctly larger and more colorful. You can gently pull the throat fan of a male out with thumb and forefinger to see it. The throat fan of a female is whitish to grayish and barely distinct from the rest of the throat, often only the thin cartilage rod being visible. Female green anoles usually have a faint, white stripe from the nape to the base of the tail.

You will want to check for ticks and mites. A tick will appear as a dark, raised, scab-like spot. Mites will look like specks of paprika or red dust. Check for these annoying pests at the bases of all the legs, around the neck, and around the eyes and vent. In short, anywhere there is a fold or cavity in the lizard's skin is a good place for ticks and mites to become established. You want to avoid bringing home an anole carrying these pests because they drain your pet anole of blood. Also, they reproduce quickly and can overwhelm your poor pet and possibly infect other reptile pets you may have at home. (The ticks and mites found on lizards do not normally bite mammals or birds.)

Female green anoles typically, but not always, have a faint white stripe on their backs.

Check the anole carefully for any sign of injury. A recently broken tail or a missing toe (there should be five on each foot) is a prime spot for infection. Although anoles can easily survive such injuries, you're better off if you start with a whole anole. Healed up stumps of toes or a regenerated tail (usually a different color than the rest of the tail) should not cause you to reject a potential pet.

Of course, you or a pet shop employee will have to handle the anole to check for parasites and injuries. The anole will not like this and should open his mouth in readiness to bite. If he does not, be suspicious. An annoyed anole is usually a healthy anole.

Stools should be firm, not runny, and there should be no visible roundworms. Greenish loose stools with a lot of mucus and/or blood mean serious problems. In general, though, you will probably have to wait until the acclimation period at home to examine stools, especially since anoles are usually housed in groups in a pet store.

Setting up a newly acquired anole by himself in a quarantine cage will help prevent him from introducing disease to any other ones you may have.

Quick & Easy Green Anole Care

If you follow the guidelines above, you should be able to purchase a healthy anole. Evaluate each animal individually, and don't be rushed. A conscientious pet shop will be just as meticulous as you are, and the staff will be happy to help. If they can't be bothered to take the time to help you, or if they won't let you examine each anole as thoroughly as described here, you might consider taking your business elsewhere; there are, after all, plenty of shops that do care.

Acclimaton

Once you've finally selected an anole or two, don't just dump them immediately into your display cage. It is often helpful to place them in a small quarantine cage for several days to a week. This lets them settle down after being crowded, poked, and prodded in the pet shop. It gives you a chance to observe them carefully under controlled conditions and perhaps to notice any possible ailments you missed before. Once you have placed them in their display cage, should they prove to be ill you may need to sterilize the cage—a lot of hassle and expense. By acclimating them in a separate enclosure you can reduce the odds of needing to fiddle with the display cage later on.

The acclimation cage can be a 5- or 10-gallon aquarium or a small mesh cage like that sold for chameleons. Plastic or silk plants will give the anoles a place to hide and also be easy to clean. Make sure to mist the anoles twice daily and feed them every day. Use newspaper or paper towels for the substrate, since this will be easy to clean and enable you to see if the feces are normal.

If you don't have extra tanks lying around, you can acclimate the anoles in what will become their regular cage. After the acclimation period of six weeks or so, remove them from the cage and place them in a gallon jar or other container (remember to use one that allows air exchange) for a couple of hours. Clean and disinfect the cage before adding the furnishings that will turn it into a nice display for you and comfortable home for your anoles. If you have assembled all the materials beforehand, you should be able to set up their display cage quickly.

Quarantine

It is best to house new reptiles in separate and fairly sterile caging for the first few months after purchase. This will allow you to observe the new pet for signs of illness and to prevent any diseases from spreading to reptiles you may already own.

The quarantine cage should be set up as described for acclimation. Make sure it is not near any other herps that you own. It would be preferable to have the quarantine cage in a separate room altogether. When performing cleaning and feeding duties, always work on your established pets first and the quarantined animals afterward. Wash your hands thoroughly after caring for the quarantined pets.

Maintain the quarantine for at least six weeks. It is even better to quarantine herps for three months. In that time period, watch carefully for signs of illness and seek veterinary assistance if anything appears amiss.

Handling Anoles

In a word: don't. Anoles, for all their charms, are not cuddly animals and really don't enjoy being handled. Obviously, there are a few times when you will have to handle your lizard, especially when you're doing some maintenance inside the cage.

If you do have to move your anole, try to grasp him right behind the head, using a thumb and forefinger. Gently! Use only enough pressure to keep the lizard from squirming and twisting his head around to bite. Close the rest of your hand softly around the body.

Wild or captive, anoles can and will bite. While they are certainly not dangerous, big anoles, such as a 7- or 8-inch male, can give you a surprisingly powerful nip, and the larger teeth at the rear of the jaws can actually draw a little bit of blood. An anole bite can be more dangerous to the lizard itself, though. Anole jaws and teeth are easily injured, especially if you try to forcibly remove the lizard from your finger. If

Quick & Easy Green Anole Care

you're bitten by an anole and he doesn't want to let go (this is pretty common), put him back in the cage still on your hand and let him get a grip on something with his feet. Usually he will then let go right away.

Anoles lose their tails very easily. This is another good reason not to handle your anoles excessively. There's always the chance you will accidentally grab the anole by the tail and it will detach. The wound left by the breaking tail, while not serious in most cases, does offer a nice spot for bacterial and fungal infections. While the tail will grow back, it will be shorter, darker in color, and often a bit kinked in comparison to the original.

There is one more reason not to handle your anole frequently, and it's the most important reason of all: handling stresses the lizard. Stress is a very subtle phenomenon that is only just starting to be appreciated as a cause of illness. Stressed animals are nervous, have poor appetites, and often fall prey to disease. There have been instances of anoles actually being killed by the stress of handling, so keep in mind that a stress-free anole is a happy anole! Keep handling to a minimum!

Collecting Anoles

Although some readers live within the green anole's natural range (or perhaps even the range of another anole species) making it possible to collect wild stock, in most cases, I would not recommend that hobbyists collect their own reptiles. In the case of the green anole I will make an exception, because they are such common reptiles over most of their range. Still, they will only stay

Handling green anoles is not recommended; it causes them a lot of stress, and they are great at escaping. This brown anole appears quite unhappy.

Stress

Stress is a word that is used frequently, but the actual meaning of the term may be less well known. The term refers to any factor that causes bodily or mental tension. Stress is so important because when living creatures suffer long-term stress, their overall health begins to decline. A system that is especially harmed by prolonged stress is the immune system, making a stressed organism more susceptible to diseases.

Obviously, you will want to give your anoles a life that is as stress free as possible. Some things that can cause stress to anoles are improper temperature and humidity, lack of climbing and hiding places, frequent handling, overcrowding, and constantly being watched (by either you or another pet, such as a cat).

common as long as people care about their welfare in the wild and their habitats remain intact, so collectors do need to follow a few simple rules.

Assuming that anoles live where you live, first make sure that it is legal to collect anoles in your area. The state fish and game department is a good place to start. Call or write them and ask whether any permits are necessary to collect anoles for personal use. If there are, get them. In some states you may need a free or inexpensive permit to keep a native reptile, while in others you must have a valid fishing or hunting license.

Second, know something about the status of anole populations in your area. For instance, if you live in southern Virginia, at the northernmost limit of the range of the green anole, don't collect them. Populations of any animal at the limit of their geographic range are often small and don't tolerate much disruption (and collecting is a disruption, however small). Don't collect if you live, for instance, in an urban area where anoles may be present but hard to find. In short, don't collect anoles unless they are very common. If they're common enough to collect in your area, you shouldn't even have to leave your backyard to find them.

Quick & Easy Green Anole Care

Finally, take only what you can use. If you are keeping anoles for the first time, collect only one or two. Don't give in to the temptation to collect a dozen just because you can. They don't do well in captivity if you crowd them.

Actually Catching an Anole

Where should you look for anoles? Check low, leafy shrubbery and small trees. Anoles often hang out on tree trunks. Even better, though, are brick walls, woodpiles, and wooden fences. When the sun hits these surfaces in the morning, you can often find anoles sunning themselves right out in the open, and if they are still a bit cold they can be easily captured by hand.

Never grab an anole by the tail. You'll only get to see a tailless lizard scurry away. Anoles' tails break off very easily as an adaptation for escaping from predators. This is called autotomy. The blood vessels at the break seal quickly, and the lizard will be none the worse for its loss. In the long run, though, he will be stressed and will burn extra energy during the regeneration period. When you're trying to catch an anole

Green anoles are often found on and around buildings within their natural range.

For the most part, green anoles stay in shrubs and on low branches, rather than climbing high into the treetops.

by hand, don't try to grab him with your fingers. Instead, try to gently slap a cupped hand over the entire lizard. It helps if you place your hand's shadow over the anole while you are still several feet away. If the shadow of your hand crosses the anole when you are closer, the lizard will probably spook.

An ideal collecting container is a cloth bag of some sort. (I like to use an old pillowcase.) Basically, you want something that's breathable and opaque. Don't use glass jars, because they are transparent, and a captured anole may become really stressed if he can see out. An old coffee can with a perforated plastic lid will work, but it can get hot on a sunny day (so can the glass jar). Transport your anole home as quickly as possible; the less time you spend out in the field, the less stressed the lizard will get. Remember to quarantine any wild-caught anole before placing him with your other pets.

Housing Your
Anole

Choosing a Cage

If there's one mistake that most beginning anole keepers make, it's not giving their pets enough room. Anoles are active and territorial, and they need a lot more space than their small size would indicate. One of the most common enclosures adapted as an anole cage is the 10-gallon aquarium, which measures 20 by 10 by 10 inches (length/width/height). Believe it or not, this cage will hold only two green anoles, and only if at least one of them is a female. Two males will bully each other mercilessly in this small space until the smaller animal weakens and dies.

Most anole species, including Jamaican giant anoles, are at least somewhat arboreal and require a tall cage that allows for climbing.

Since anoles are so arboreal, even the 10-gallon tank is not ideal. It will work for an anole or two, but if you really want to enjoy viewing your pets, give them a tank that is not just roomy, but tall. In a tall tank, they will do a lot of climbing, and you'll get to see a lot of acrobatic jumping. A 20-gallon "high" tank, measuring 24 by 12 by 26 inches, makes an excellent house for a pair or trio of anoles. If you'd really like to keep more anoles, move up to a 55-gallon tank. Measuring a hefty 48 by 13 by 20 inches, it will comfortably house a male and three or four females. You may be able to house two males, but you must be watchful that they do not fight. To help prevent fighting, introduce both males to the cage at the same time and have basking lights, water bowls, and hiding places at both ends.

Another alternative is to use the finely meshed fabric enclosures designed to keep chameleons. These are vertical enclosures supported by plastic poles with the mesh zipping around the frame. They are designed to house a plant or two and often have a shallow pan that collects drippings from regular mistings at their base. These enclosures are very light in weight (compared to the massive, fragile nature of a large aquarium tank), inexpensive, easy to move from inside to outside when the weather permits, and fairly durable. They have a lot to offer a pair of anoles or a male and his harem of three or four females.

Substrates

There are several possible substrates for the floor of the terrarium. The ideal substrate will retain some moisture, since green anoles need about 50 to 60 percent relative humidity. Anoles kept in dry terraria will get dehydrated. Pet stores formerly recommended gravel as a substrate for most reptiles, but it is a poor choice for most species, especially anoles. It does not hold humidity well, and wastes tend to sink down underneath, forming a breeding ground for bacteria. Sand is also not good, because it can irritate the toes of anoles by getting between the ridges. Also, anoles kept over sand may end up accidentally ingesting some that is stuck to moist food. This can be dangerous, causing blockages to the digestive tract. Like gravel, sand is poor at holding humidity.

Corncob, sometimes recommended as a reptile bedding, is a terrible substrate. It looks very unnatural. The biggest drawback, however, is that when it gets wet, it turns into a disgusting mess that readily harbors mold and bacteria. If that's not enough to turn you off corn-

Sphagnum moss over a substrate of potting soil will work well for green anoles in a naturalistic setup.

Housing Your Anole

Perlite Is Bad

Many potting soils contain a material called perlite, which is a granular white material of mineral origin. Others contain little particles of Styrofoam. These materials are added to increase drainage and aeration of the soil. While these materials are good for plants, they can cause problems for your lizards. Both perlite and Styrofoam can cause gut impactions, which can be fatal to your anoles. It is best to buy potting soils that do not contain these materials. Unfortunately, most potting soils contain one or the other, but organic potting soils should contain neither. Therefore, it is best to use organic potting soils for substrates and in the pots of any plants you place in your anole enclosure.

cob, it has been implicated in causing gut impactions—serious blockages—in reptiles.

Potting soil or topsoil is a good substrate if the cage is heavily planted. You do have to be careful not to get it too wet, but the plants will help to recycle some anole waste matter. Use organic potting soil to avoid possibly poisoning your anole with fertilizers or other additives. Soil substrates work best when you use a one-inch deep layer of gravel under the soil; this provides some drainage. Potting soil is easier to work with if you mix it with sand; make a mixture that is about 25 percent sand.

One of the best anole substrates is bark mulch. Some say that orchid bark is preferable to other types, but I've had good luck keeping a variety of reptiles and amphibians on pine bark mulch. Bark mulch will retain a good deal of humidity, but it is also loose enough that air circulates well through it, keeping stagnant spots to a minimum. A relatively thin layer of topsoil under a generous quantity of bark mulch will give live plants a friendly environment in which to take root.

Aspen and pine shavings, while useful for other species of herps, are not a good choice for anoles or other animals that need relatively high humidity. The shavings get soggy quickly and grow mold.

Recycled paper bedding is a good choice for most herps including anoles. It holds humidity well, is nonabrasive, and can be composted or flushed down the toilet. It does tend to be expensive, but is otherwise a fine bedding.

Plants and Branches

Make plenty of allowance for the arboreal nature of your anoles. They don't appreciate being earthbound. Lots of wooden limbs and branches should be placed in the terrarium, and they should run at all angles—front to back, top to bottom, side to side. They not only provide needed exercise equipment for the anoles to run and jump around on, but they also serve as convenient territorial boundary markers. You'll see how this works as your anoles select a favorite branch or group of branches. Although they don't spend a great deal of time on the ground, you can make the floor of the terrarium interesting by adding rocks and logs.

Vines

One of the many products manufactured for herps is artificial vines. There are a number of different types. Any of them make naturalistic and functional decorations for your anole cage. Some are poseable, allowing you to shape them as you like. They can greatly increase the number of climbing and basking surfaces your anoles can use.

A warning if you use artificial vines: Some types have a flexible wire inside. As the vine ages, the wire can break through the surface. Periodically check the vine; if you see the wire poking out, discard it before it injures your anoles.

Plants are a lot of fun. Your anole terrarium can be a miniature garden, and if you have a green thumb there are lots of possibilities open to you. However, it is not a good idea to stick the plant in the cage right from the store. First, take the plant out of its pot and rinse the plant and its roots off. Rinse away as much of the dirt as possible. This helps get rid of any pesticides or fertilizers that might have been used on the plant plus eliminates any undesirable critters— mainly ants and centipedes—that might be living in the soil. Then, repot the plant in fresh soil and a new pot. The plant is now ready to be added to your vivarium. You can keep the plant in a pot, or, if using a potting soil substrate, plant it directly in the substrate.

One of the best plants you could pick is a philodendron (also called pothos). They're pretty—one variety even has leaves that are variegated in green and gold—plus they are almost indestructible. Plant a small philodendron in each rear corner of the terrarium and you will quickly see them fill in the remaining space. Their leaves will also vine around the exposed branches, giving them a more lively appearance. You will soon have to prune back the philodendrons, but the cuttings root easily in water and can then be potted to give to friends or added to other herp enclosures.

One of the best plants for a green anole enclosure is pothos. It is hardy, pretty, and nontoxic.

Quick & Easy Green Anole Care

Another good plant is English ivy. The indented leaves are interesting in shape. Ivy grows with amazing speed and also has a creeping habit, winding around bare branches. The leaves are not quite as tough as those of a philodendron, but they are tough enough for small lizards like anoles. This is another plant you will have to prune on a regular schedule.

Designing a naturalistic terrarium for your green anole is challenging, but the result can be an interesting addition to your home.

One more creeping plant that is nice for contrast is wandering Jew, which has attractive green and purple leaves. It tends to grow along the ground more than the others and probably won't climb to the same extent.

One plant I particularly like is schefflera. There are "big-leaf" and "small-leaf" varieties. The big-leaf is a good-sized plant that won't fit into any but the largest terraria, so you should probably go with the small-leaf variety. The five-part compound leaves are bright green. The leaf stalks grow vertically or horizontally, and the plant is not a creeper; rather, it will form a small bush. The leaves of scheffleras are particularly springy—great for the active anoles.

Bromeliads are excellent in the anole terrarium. Many nurseries refer to bromeliads as "air plants." Most do not root in the soil, but instead attach themselves (non-parasitically) to tree limbs or bark.

Housing Your Anole

Small bromeliads can be anchored to wooden branches with rubber bands. In time, they will attach firmly and the rubber bands can be removed.

There are many other plant possibilities. Get a houseplant book and visit a local greenhouse, and you will certainly get some terrific ideas for landscaping your terrarium. Just be sure to select plants that will survive in the cage conditions and that won't pose a threat to your anoles.

Other Equipment

Somewhere in the cage you should have a thermometer and hygrometer (which measures relative humidity). There are electronic models that will give you digital readouts on panels mounted on the front of the terrarium, with their small sensors hidden inconspicuously behind plants or other decor. These models are often expensive, though, and many of you will prefer the less expensive ones with a dial and needle. It's up to you, but it is important to be able to monitor both temperature and humidity accurately. Recently some small battery-operated units with many features have become widely available at reasonable prices.

The final step of setting up the inside of the terrarium is to get a wire mesh lid. The mesh squares should be one-quarter inch. Anything larger may let the anoles escape or, even worse, get stuck halfway. Smaller mesh may also trap them. Aluminum window screening is especially bad. Anoles will sometimes snag a toenail in it to the point that they pull off a toe when struggling to free themselves.

Lights

Now that the housing is decorated and covered, we can consider the vital topics of light and heat, which overlap to some degree, as you'll see.

Anoles require proper humidity for healthy skin shedding. Bahaman brown anoles, like green anoles, require 50 to 60 percent relative humidity.

Just above the cage lid, across the entire length of the cage, you should run a full-spectrum fluorescent light. These tubes closely mimic the spectrum of natural sunlight. Most importantly, in the full-spectrum fluorescent tubes is a type of light you can't even see: ultraviolet (UV). UV light is high-energy radiation that helps reptiles synthesize their own vitamin D3, which is intimately tied to calcium metabolism and thus promotes healthy bones and teeth, among other things. It should be noted, however, that all fluorescent tubes degrade with time. In general, you should replace the tubes about every six months, but refer to the manufacturer's specifications to be absolutely sure. Be sure to buy a UV light made for reptiles that produces ultraviolet B waves. It is the ultraviolet B waves that actually allow animals to synthesize vitamin D.

Basking Light

In addition to the fluorescent light, you must provide an incandescent light as a source of heat. It should shine over only one corner. This lets the anoles regulate their internal temperature by moving away to the cool end of the cage if necessary. Use a spotlight, as a normal, round bulb does not concentrate the heat over one area as

In nature, anoles obtain heat from basking in the sunlight, so they require heat lamps when kept as pets.

effectively. The wattage of the bulb will depend on the size of the cage. You will have to experiment to see what bulb maintains the proper temperature. Aim the spotlight at a large branch or rock that can serve as a basking site. You will need a thermometer to measure the air temperature at the basking site. It should be about 90°F. Of course, the basking light must be mounted outside the lid of the cage or it will certainly burn the anoles. Even minor burns can be fatal to a small lizard like an anole. Never place a light bulb of any type within the terrarium.

The air temperature over the rest of the terrarium should be about 72 to 80°F. The warmth radiating from the basking spotlight and the fluorescent lights will probably do this effectively, but if you need to boost the temperature a bit more, you can add a second incandescent light—the normal round variety—to spread out the heat a little more. Having one thermometer at the basking site and other at the opposite end of the cage is recommended. Keep the cage away from drafty areas, but you can let the temperature drop to as low as 60 to 65°F by night. Green anoles can safely tolerate the occasional temperature drop to 50°F

Quick & Easy Green Anole Care

if they can warm up sufficienly during the day. Such lows are not recommended.

Photoperiod

The length of the day is one of the factors anoles use to set their "biological clocks." (Remember the pineal eye!) For most of the year you should keep the lights on for 14 hours a day.

Automatic timers—easily found in any hardware store—will make photoperiod regulation a breeze. Trust me, it can become a hassle to remember to turn on the lights at the same time every day. If you're inconsistent about the length of time the lights are on each day, the anoles can get confused, for lack of a better term. They may go off their feed, and if the situation continues, they may take ill from the stress.

Minimalistic Cages

If your funds are limited, or if you prefer a simpler cage to make maintenance easier, here are some tips. Set up the cage using only a 1- to 2-inch layer of bark mulch as a substrate, with no underlying

New Type of Bulb

There are now incandescent bulbs that supply ultraviolet B. These tend to be expensive, but they last a long time, so long that it is more economical in the long term to buy these instead of a fluorescent bulb that will need to be replaced every six months or so. The problem with these bulbs is that they generate a lot of heat and do not normally come in wattages lower than 60 watts. This means that if your anole cage is small (under 20 gallons), they may make it too hot for your lizards. These UV incandescents are otherwise excellent products. You can find them on the Internet and at pet stores that have good reptile supply sections.

No Heat Rocks

Many pet stores that are inexperienced with reptiles recommend electrically heated artificial rocks (usually called hot rocks or heat rocks) for use with anoles. There are many reason why these are not just unnecessary but dangerous for anoles and other arboreal lizards: the rocks only heat a small spot of the cage, not the air; over time, these rocks sometimes develop spots that are much hotter than they should be, creating a risk of serious burns; if you use one as your main source of heat, your anole will sit on the rock all the time, which will eventually cause burns; lastly, anoles are adapted to have heat come down on them from the sun and may not recognize a hot rock as a heat source.

Because of these reasons, hot rocks are a bad idea to include in the cage of most reptiles and are certainly dangerous for anoles. Do not use them.

topsoil. Plants are still necessary, but they can be in clay pots to make removal easy. You could also get by with fake plants. You can use just the full-spectrum light, and eliminate the heat lamp. Extra heat can be supplied by placing an aquarium heater in a gallon jar filled with water, then placing this combo in the terrarium. Be careful not to let the water inside the jar get much over 90°F, and make sure to top off the water inside the jar as it evaporates, as an aquarium heater exposed to air overheats and cracks in just minutes.

Outdoor Enclosures

If you live in an area that experiences good anole temperatures for at least part of the year, you might want to build an outdoor enclosure for your anoles. You can construct a simple frame with plywood and then staple quarter-inch mesh hardware cloth to the framework. (Make sure there are no sharp edges, and that the door fits securely enough to prevent the anoles from escaping.) There are several advantages here. One is that you can build a large enclosure very cheaply. Another is that you will probably not have to feed your anoles very frequently. A dish of fruit placed in the cage will attract many flies and other insects on which the anoles can feast. You will also not have to worry about artificial lighting and heat, but do make sure the cage is not out in full sun for the whole day. It is better to place it in light shade, where shafts of sunlight penetrate here and there. Several large potted plants will give the anoles shelter, and they will likely lay their eggs in soil in the pots. (Collect the eggs promptly, though, because the hatchlings will probably be able to slip through the mesh if they hatch inside the cage.) The disadvantage to this setup is that you have little control over your lizards—they are subject to all the possible parasites and harsh environmental conditions encountered by their wild brethren. In general, I recommend that you try an outdoor cage only if you live in an area where green anoles are native, just in case they or their offspring escape in spite of all of your precautions.

Maintenance

Regardless of the type of cage layout you select, there will be some maintenance required. Remove fecal matter as soon as you see it. (Even in a naturalistic cage you should be able to find almost all of it.) I like to replace small areas of substrate with fresh material on a rotating basis. For instance, one month you might change the substrate in the right one-third of the terrarium, the next month the center one-third, and so on. This way, even if you miss some waste material, and even if the plants do not recycle all of it, you will have reduced the chances of having the cage become unsanitary.

Monitor the temperature and humidity every day. You may find that condensation builds up on the inside glass; the water may also leave spots on the glass. When necessary, you can remove it simply by wiping evenly from top to bottom with a paper towel.

Feed every day in most cases, or at least every other day. Look for anole eggs buried in the soil and remove them to incubators. Spend

Cleaners Can Kill

Never use ammonia-based window cleaners, or any other cleaning fluid, in or near your anole cage. The risk of accidentally poisoning your lizards is just too great. Also, avoid spraying air fresheners or home disinfectants near the cage.

If you want to disinfect the cage, use a solution of 10 percent bleach and water. Rinse thoroughly (until no scent of bleach remains) and allow to air dry before putting your anoles back in the cage.

a few minutes watching the anoles every day to make sure they are active, alert, and acting normally. Don't shirk your responsibilities; just a few minutes of care each day will greatly reduce the chances of problems later on.

When properly cared for, a naturalistic anole cage is a beautiful accent to your home (or yard) and is even pretty enough to go right into the living room.

Feeding Your Anole

Feeding anoles is not difficult, but there are some tricks to making sure that your anole gets the right kind of food and enough of it.

Insects, Insects, Insects

Anoles are insect-eating lizards and rarely consume anything else. In the past, pet stores often told customers that anoles ate earthworms or dried flies. Rarely will an anole eat an earthworm, and they usually don't recognize food that isn't moving. So, most of these poor anoles would eventually starve to death

Store employees have become more educated and usually recom-

Anoles eat a variety of small insects in the wild. This one has caught a moth.

mend crickets and/or mealworms as anole food. Unfortunately, they don't normally discuss food size or balanced diets—two important subjects. And, pet stores often recommend feeding anoles only once or twice a week, which is not nearly frequently enough.

The rest of this chapter will tell you everything you need to know about feeding your anole properly. This will go a long way toward ensuring he lives a long and happy life.

Variety Is the Spice of Life

Even for anoles, variety in the diet seems to be important. By feeding your anoles a diversity of feeder insects, you help ensure that they are getting all the proper nutrients that they need. If you feed only one type of insect for every meal, it is very possible that that particular insect is deficient in one nutrient or another. By feeding a diet of diverse insects, you make it less likely that any one nutrient is being left out. Additionally, it seems that variety stimulates the appetite of anoles and other herps. This makes sense; wouldn't you get bored if you could only eat one food all of the time?

Quick & Easy Green Anole Care

Crickets

Crickets, *Acheta domestica*, are probably the most popular live food for insectivores, and they are one of the best. In spite of the debate over whether crickets or mealworms are digested more efficiently by lizards, it does seem that fewer cases of digestive upset result from an exclusive diet of crickets as opposed to one of mealworms. In hardiness, ease of handling, and overall nutritive value, I prefer to use crickets.

Another plus to crickets is that they are fast moving. Active insects are really attractive to anoles, and the psychological benefit of the chase should not be overlooked. It really does invigorate anoles to run around after their prey, and the activity reduces stress. The bottom line is that exercise is as good for your anoles as it is for you and me. Crickets are available from your pet shop in a wide variety of sizes, from "pinheads" on up to adults about an inch long. An appropriately sized cricket should be about half the length of your anole's head, although your lizards will try to cram down larger ones. Eating food that is too large for them can cause anoles to vomit or even cause an internal injury.

Mealworms

Mealworms, *Tenebrio* sp., are the larvae of a small black beetle. They

Crickets are readily available at most pet stores and can make up the majority of the green anole diet.

are easily maintained and bred in a medium consisting of grain-based foods: oats, cornflakes, etc. The medium must be kept pretty dry, or fungal infections can kill off the whole mealworm colony. Mealworms are pretty slow moving, and not all anoles will take them. They also have a lot of chitin (shell or exoskeleton), and if fed in large quantities can prove hard to digest. The adult beetles can also be fed to your anoles, but they are hard-shelled and have a lot less food value than the mealworms they developed from. Also, many anoles just won't eat the beetles.

Don't just toss mealworms around the cage and hope your anoles will find them. Most of the mealworms will burrow into the substrate and escape. Place a dozen or so in a steep-sided glass dish that is buried flush with the substrate. It will take them a little while to get used to it, but eventually your anoles will learn that this is where the food is, and they'll look for the mealworms in the dish.

Roaches (Yes, Roaches)

Cockroaches are pretty disgusting, if you ask me. Still, small roaches such as the German cockroach, *Blatella germanica*, are fast moving, and anoles really seem to enjoy chasing them down. They are very easy to raise and eat just about anything, but because of the danger of infesting your house with them, they are better if not used for herp food. At some reptile shows or through Internet suppliers, you may find various small roaches for sale, such as Cuban green roaches, *Panchlora nivea*, or lobster roaches, *Nauphoeta cinerea*. These tropical roaches have a much smaller chance of infesting your home, and most herpers brave enough to try roaches highly recommend them as a food source.

Waxworms

Waxworms, *Galleria mellonella*, are the larvae of a small moth and inhabit abandoned beehives. They can be raised on a mixture of beeswax, honey, and oats. Like mealworms, waxworms are slow moving, but they have much softer bodies. Feed them to your lizards in a dish. The adult moths are a special treat and will give your anoles a good workout as they chase them around the cage. Note that waxworms are high in fat and low in other nutrients. Use them as an occasional food, not a staple.

Gut-loading

A cricket, or any other food insect, is only as nutritious as its gut contents. When a lizard eats a tasty mealworm, he not only is eating the mealworm but also all of the food that is still being digested by the mealworm. This partially digested food is an important source of nutrition for the lizard. The most important thing is not so much what you feed the lizard, but what you feed to the food the lizard eats.

Crickets are a good example because they are usually poorly fed at pet stores—making them nutritionally poor for your lizard—but will eat nearly anything, making them fairly easy to gut-load. To

Fruit Flies

If you eventually breed your anoles (and I do hope you'll try), you will need some very tiny foods for the hatchlings. To provide these tiny creatures with food, the easiest method is to raise wingless fruit flies. Fruit fly larvae will eat almost any sort of sweet, overripe fruit, but it is much less messy to order both the flies and a culture medium from a mail order dealer (pet shops don't often carry them, but it wouldn't hurt to check).

You will feed the fruit flies by opening the container over the cage and dumping some in. Close the container quickly, or many flies will run up and out. To reduce the number of flies that wander out of the cage, put a small piece of sweet fruit—banana, peach, or something similar—in a dish or bottle cap on the floor of the cage. The flies mostly will stay on the fruit.

make them a better lizard food, we want to boost their protein, vitamin C, and calcium content (along with smaller amounts of many other vitamins and minerals). There are several possible sources of protein, and some keepers suggest the use of finely crushed rodent food. Another source is tropical fish flake food. The dry food will get them pretty thirsty, so give them a wedge of fresh orange (adds vitamin C and calcium). They will also eat grated carrot (adds vitamin A and calcium) or leafy greens, such as collards, dandelions, or kale (add many vitamins, calcium, and other minerals). Crickets will eat lots of other vegetable matter, so be imaginative. Here are just a few ideas: sprouts, zucchini, summer squash, melon, sweet potato, and berries of all kinds.

There are also cricket foods available on the market. These work well for most keepers and are gradually replacing, at least in part, more traditional methods of feeding crickets.

Keep your crickets in a glass gallon jar, a small aquarium (dry, of course), or one of those small plastic animal cages that the pet shops sell (the kind with the slotted plastic tops). Good ventilation is important. High humidity kills crickets in droves. Gut-load the crickets for at least 24 hours before you offer them to your anoles. Keeping the food in small, shallow dishes in the cricket cage will make cleaning much easier.

To load up your mealworms, just feed a nutritious diet to your colony. Use a mix of oatmeal, rice baby cereal, wheat germ, or other nutritious grain-based foods. Roaches can be gut-loaded just like crickets. Because of their specialized diet, waxworms are difficult to gut-load.

Supplements

It is a good idea to provide vitamin and mineral supplements to your anoles. The powdered forms are the best, because these can easily be added to crickets and other feeder insects. Take four or five crickets and place them in a small plastic bag. Place about a teaspoon of powdered reptile vitamin/mineral supplement into the bag (your pet shop can offer you several good brands, but make sure they are formulated specifically for reptiles and amphibians). Gently shake the crickets around in the bag until they are well coated with the vitamin powder. You should use the supplements with about one feeding each week, maybe twice that with a baby anole.

I realize that all this must seem like a lot of trouble to go through to prepare your lizards' food, but it really is not a big deal once you get used to it. Plus, it is an absolute necessity for keeping your herps healthy, so it is well worth the effort.

Wild Foods

You can collect insects from your yard or other wild spaces if you are careful. The first thing you must do is be sure that you are collecting from an area that has not been sprayed or treated with any pesticides, fungicides, fertilizers, weed killers, or other toxins. You don't want to harm your anoles by exposing them to nasty chemicals. You must remember to feed only insects that are the proper size—nothing too big.

Be careful of what insects you collect. Some could be dangerous for your anoles. These would include centipedes, which have a nasty bite, and large spiders. Avoid any

Larger species of anoles, like Cuban knight anoles, need larger prey than green anoles. Try large roaches, silkworms, tomato hornworms, and baby mice.

insects that are brightly colored; such colors usually advertise toxicity. Do not feed any caterpillars that are fuzzy or spiky. Some invertebrates that are good for your lizards to eat are pill bugs, flies, inchworms, katydids, moths, small grasshoppers, and small spiders.

Lastly, you should understand that when you feed wild-collected prey, there is a slight risk of introducing parasites to your pets. As long as your anoles behave normally and are not losing weight, everything should be fine. If they are sluggish, not eating, losing weight, or have worms or worm eggs in their stools, you should take them to the vet for treatment. It is unlikely that feeding wild-caught bugs will cause a problem, but it is best to know that it might and be prepared just in case.

Fruits, Too

Although green anoles really like their bugs, they will occasionally consume some vegetable matter, particularly sweet, fruity stuff. A fruit puree makes a good treat. Take a soft fruit such as a plum, peach, or banana, and add some vitamin powder and a bit of honey. Puree it well in a blender (add some water if the mixture is too thick). When you're done, the mix should be about the consistency of a thick milkshake. When the "fruit shake" is placed in a shallow dish, anoles will often lap at it. Use it sparingly, and don't let it sit more than a day—it goes bad pretty fast.

How Much?

Our last food-related points are important ones: how much do you feed your anole, and how often? It's difficult to give you absolute answers to these questions, but in general, an adult anole will consume four or five medium-sized crickets, or their equivalents (mealworms, etc.), every day to every other day. One way to know whether you're overfeeding your anole is if it eats well for several days but then suddenly stops eating. If this happens, let the lizard go hungry for a day and then feed a little less in the future (one or two fewer insects per feeding). You will find that if you can feed at

Green anoles will sometimes eat soft fruits, including berries. Many anoles will eat bananas mashed with honey and vitamins.

the same time every day and at roughly the same spot in the cage (easy if you use a dish), your anoles will anticipate feeding time and stand ready at the feeding station.

Water

Water is as important as food. Anoles drink a lot of it. The problem is, they won't drink it from a bowl. Just as they like active food, they seem to enjoy "chasing" their water as well!

An anole will probably drink, on average, about a half tea-spoon of water per day. There are several ways to supply this water. Placing an aquarium air-stone (connected to a small air pump) into a water bowl will splash small droplets on the nearby glass sides of the cage and on plant leaves. The anoles

Green anoles drink by lapping up droplets of dew or rain. Spray your anoles with a plant mister to provide them with drinking water. Misting also helps maintain proper humidity.

Some anoles will drink from a water bowl. Keep the water bowl clean, because dirty water can make your anoles sick.

will lick at droplets that catch the light and shine. The down side to this method is that it can be tough to get the splash rate just right; you don't want to soak the whole area around the bowl.

Probably the most common method of supplying water is to mist the tank two or more times daily. Using a clean spray bottle—never one that has ever contained cleaners or chemicals—lightly wet the plant leaves and the glass sides of the terrarium. Getting the anoles wet doesn't hurt either. The down side is the same as before—don't soak the terrarium. A wet terrarium is a breeding place for bacterial and fungal diseases. When you mist the cage, it should look like a light dew, not like a rain shower.

Additionally, commercial drip and misting systems of varying complexity and expense are widely available today, as they are used to maintain true chameleons, which are even more sensitive to moving water than anoles.

Quick & Easy Green Anole Care

Breeding Anoles

Once you have gotten pretty good at keeping anoles, you may be curious about how to breed them. Breeding anoles is not too difficult, although raising the hatchlings can be tricky because of their small size.

Sexes

Sexing adult anoles is not difficult. Male green anoles can reach about 9 inches in total length, while the females generally run about 2 inches shorter. Of course, the male has a brightly colored throat fan, and the female's fan is generally white and much less developed than the male's. Males also have enlarged postanal (behind the vent) scales with a row of pores on the underside.

Careful Cooling

Either sex may have a white stripe down the center of the back, but this tends to fade in adult males and is more distinct in juveniles and adult females. We already know that males with the reddest throat fans are most successful in securing territories, but they also get the most females. Research has shown that females prefer males with the brightest pink throat fans; males with a more greenish or whitish fan are pretty much out of luck if a pink-dewlapped guy is in the neighborhood.

Cycling

In the wild, green anoles go into a period of dormancy in autumn. In the northern part of their range, they enter true hibernation, but in most areas it tends to be a state of brumation. This means the anoles will still come out on warm days, but will spend days to several weeks in dormancy. For anoles to breed successfully in captivity, a brumation period is essential.

About October, reduce feedings, and after a couple of weeks, stop feedings altogether. Concurrently, start gradually reducing the photoperiod and temperature. Basically, you're trying to convince the anoles' biological clocks that winter has arrived. After several weeks you want the cage day length to be only eight hours long and the temperature only about 65 to 70°F during the day and 50 to 60°F at night. You will probably not see much of the anoles—don't disturb them. You can try to offer food if they come out, but don't get upset if they don't eat. If you fed them well beforehand, they should have sufficient fat reserves to weather the winter. After four to six weeks of this treatment you can begin to reverse the process—again, do it gradually, over several weeks.

Quick & Easy Green Anole Care

During breeding season, green anoles may mate several times a day. The female will lay one egg about every two weeks.

Soon you will be back to the normal 12- to 14-hour day and the temperatures in the 80s, and you can get the anoles back on their regular feeding schedule. You should soon notice courtship behavior in your lizards. A male will approach a female with dewlap erect and the head bobbing. The female will probably attempt to run away, but the male will follow her, attempting to stay in a parallel position. If he can catch her (and the ability to catch her signals that the female is receptive), he will bite at the nape of her neck and hold on. At this point both lizards will stop, and the male will wrap his body tightly around his mate's. Most importantly, he will get his tail and vent region wrapped under hers and soon will insert one of his

The More, the Merrier

If you are keeping one male and one female anole, you may find that the male never leaves the female alone and is always trying to mate with her. To prevent the male from overly harassing the female—and keeping her from eating and resting properly—it sometimes helps to have several females. This allows the male to spread his attention out over a few females, and no single female gets constantly bothered. Just be sure to not overcrowd your anoles.

Breeding Anoles

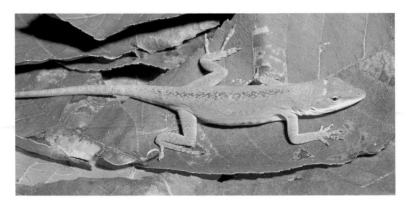

Green anole females make a simple nest. They just deposit eggs under leaf litter or shallowly in the dirt.

hemipenes (lizards and snakes have the penis divided into two lobes) into her cloaca (vent) for sperm transfer. Mating will last about five minutes. Mating may be repeated numerous times in the days to follow, but fertilization can occur after only one mating.

Females can store sperm and lay fertile eggs for the entire breeding season, which may last four to five months. In the wild, it's roughly May to September, but by altering temperature and photoperiod you can breed anoles almost any time you wish.

Laying

After mating, it is very important to make sure the female anole gets enough calcium, which will be used to make eggshells. About two weeks after mating, the female should be noticeably heavier and a little bit sluggish. She will look for a moist, warm spot in the substrate and will dig a small hole with her head. In the hole she will lay one egg (rarely two). She will then push the egg into the hole with her snout and cover it up with soil. You have to be very observant, or you may miss the event. Look carefully for the female's sudden slimness, then search the substrate for signs of digging. Two weeks later, the sequence will repeat. The female will lay approximately ten eggs in the course of one breeding season. If the terrarium is humid enough the eggs can be left in the terrarium.

Breeding Other Anoles

Most of the commonly available anole species can be bred in a similar fashion to green anoles. However, the tropical species should never be subjected to temperatures below 70°F. The exact temperatures for incubating the eggs and the length of incubation will vary by species. If you are interested in breeding other species of anoles, you should research the needs of the species and the eggs carefully before starting.

Incubation

For the sake of control, it is best to remove the eggs to an incubator. A plastic shoebox filled with barely damp vermiculite or sterile sand is ideal. Bury the eggs halfway in the incubator substrate. It is important to position the eggs as they were found. Unlike bird eggs, reptile eggs do not like to be rotated, and inverting the egg may damage or kill the embryo. It is also important for the incubator box to stay at an even temperature of 82°F. Low light levels are best for developing eggs, and a warm closet will often suffice as the place to put the incubator box. Check the eggs once or twice a week to make sure none have gone bad.

Breeders tend to focus their efforts on the uncommon anoles. This is a hatchling Jamaican giant anole.

At 82°F, the eggs will hatch in 40 days, give or take a few. The hatchlings will be about 2 to 2.5 inches long. They will mature at 4 to 5 inches total length, and they can reach this size in only a few months. In the wild, green anoles breed at an age of about one year. Green anoles should be able to breed for several years.

A rare but naturally occurring variety of green anoles is actually blue. Breeders propagate this variety and charge more for them than for the normal ones.

Hatchlings

Hatchlings must be fed copious quantities of tiny foods, such as wingless fruit flies, meadow plankton—tiny insects caught by sweeping a net through grasses and other foliage—and pinhead-sized crickets. They must also have a great deal of calcium to support normal bone development considering their rapid growth rate. They will require two to three times as much calcium as a full-grown adult. Dust their insects with vitamin supplements; it is also recommended to feed the hatchlings fruit puree that the vitamin/mineral supplement has been added to. As with the adults, make sure the babies are kept under full-spectrum lighting.

When the young males begin to display, it is time to begin dividing up the young anoles, or bitter fighting will soon ensue. You can trade them with your friends or the members of a local herp society. Your pet shop may also be interested in your homegrown anoles. Admittedly, you'll never get rich breeding anoles, but it is a rewarding endeavor.

Other Anoles

There are over 300 species of anoles ranging from the southeastern US south over the northern half of South America and occurring on most of the islands of the Caribbean. Additionally, many anoles not otherwise native to the US have become established in Florida, Hawaii, and possibly other states. It should not come as a surprise that anoles other than the green anole can be found in the pet trade. Most of them are as interesting and pretty—if not more so—than the green anole and make rewarding captives. A few of these species are being bred by hobbyists. In fact, in the European herp hobby, anoles are rather popular. Occasionally, rare and strange anoles bred by European hobbyists become available in the US hobby. If

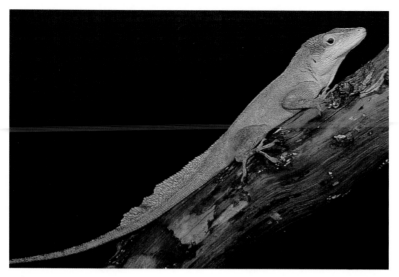

The Marie Galante sail-tailed anole has been found in Florida but does not appear to be established yet.

you have an interest in these anoles, you would do best buying them when you see them, as the availability of captive-bred, oddball anoles is unstable.

Most of the anoles we'll discuss in this chapter can be kept in similar conditions as the green anole. Since they are all more tropical in origin than our green friend, they should not be exposed to low temperatures. Unless stated otherwise, do not expose these anole species to temperatures lower than 70°F.

Bark anoles are small anoles that resemble house geckos. They have been established in Florida for over 50 years.

Anoles in Florida

Among the nonnative animals now calling the Sunshine State home are at least 10 species of anoles, according to the Florida Fish and Wildlife Conservation Commission. Of the following anoles, all but two, *Anolis extremus* and *A. ferreus*, are established and breeding.

Barbados Anole, *Anolis extremus*

Bark Anole, *Anolis distichus*

Brown Anole, *Anolis sagrei*

Cuban Green Anole, *Anolis porcatus*

Hispaniolan Green Anole, *Anolis chlorocyanus*

Knight Anole, *Anolis equestris*

Largehead Anole, *Anolis cybotes*

Marie Galante Sail-tailed Anole, *Anolis ferreus*

Puerto Rican Crested Anole, *Anolis cristatellus*

Jamaican Giant Anole, *Anolis garmani*

Bark Anole

This small anole, *A. distichus*, occurs in at least 17 subspecies found on many islands in the Bahamas as well as on parts of the island of Hispaniola. The Florida population is derived from several different subspecies introduced over many years. It was first documented in Florida over 50 years ago.

Bark anoles are rarely more than five inches long. They are fast and agile with a spindly appearance. The color of the dewlap varies greatly among the different subspecies. The overall color is a lichen-like pattern of grays and browns. This little anole may fare well in a cage with green anoles, but it is possible the larger anoles would eat or out-compete them.

Brown Anole

Brown anoles, *A. sagrei*, are probably the second most popular anole

Like in green anoles, male brown anoles are larger than the females and have a more prominent dewlap. A female is pictured above, a male below.

in the hobby. They are often sold as Bahaman brown anoles or just Bahaman anoles. As the name suggests, they are found in the Bahamas, but also on many other Caribbean Islands including Cuba, Jamaica, the Caymans, and the Turks and Caicos Islands. They have been established in Florida for quite some time and in some areas appear to be replacing the native green anole.

Brown anoles are aptly named, as they are always some shade of brown. There are often yellowish or whitish markings (some populations have reddish or orange diamonds) on the back. Males have a

Puerto Rican crested anoles are now established and breeding in Florida.

thickened nape and a crest on the tail. The dewlap is bright red or reddish orange with a white border. A male may reach a little more than eight inches in total length, while the females are considerably smaller.

This is one of the best species for the pet hobbyist. It is active and hardy. They tend to be more terrestrial than green anoles and stay on the ground or close to it. In a tall cage, they can be kept with green anoles. The two species will divide the space, with the green anoles staying at the top and the brown anoles hanging around the bottom. Brown anoles can tolerate nighttime temperatures as low as 60°F.

Crested Anole

Anolis cristatellus reaches about seven inches in length and is brownish in coloration. Male crested anoles have a high crest on the tail and a greenish to pale tan dewlap. Females are smaller, somewhat more slender, and lack the crest. This is another anole that has been introduced and is established in Florida. In Florida, it is sometimes confused with the brown anole and the largehead anole. Crested anoles are native to Puerto Rico and neighboring islands.

This anole can be kept with green anoles, brown anoles, and other species of similar size and habits.

Other Anoles   59

Jamaican Giant Anole

Unlike the anoles we've discussed up to this point, Jamaican giant anoles, *A. garmani*, are sizable lizards. Males may reach over a foot in total length, with females roughly two-thirds the size of the males. A beautiful and impressive species, this anole is bright green with a crest of erect spines on the nape and back. This crest extends down to the tail in males and some females. Females may have brownish vertical bands on the body. The dewlap is pale to deep orange with a pale olive border. This anole is native to Jamaica but has become established in Florida.

This is a nervous and aggressive species (watch your fingers) that does best in a tall, heavily planted cage, where it will spend most of its time hiding in the foliage at the top of the cage. In time, Jamaican giants will become more comfortable and stop spending so much time hiding. Do not house with other species, and certainly never house two males together. One male can be kept with up to three females, provided the cage is large enough (at least 3 ft by 3 ft by 3 ft).

Knight Anole

The knight anole, *A. equestris,* is a truly giant species with males reaching almost 24 inches in length. There are a number of subspecies, some of which are undoubtedly distinct species. Knight anoles are native to

Odd anoles sometimes turn up in the herp hobby. The beautiful Allison's anole, A. allisoni, *from Cuba, only appears in the hobby rarely.*

Captive-bred knight anoles can be tame and handledable, while the wild-caught ones are normally fierce and aggressive.

Cuba, but they have been introduced to Florida, Hawaii, Jamaica, and other Caribbean Islands. Healthy individuals are bright green with a cream to yellow stripe extending back from the base of the front leg to mid-body and usually bright yellow lips. The dewlap is pink to white and well developed in both males and females.

Knight anoles are often in bad shape when they are found in pet shops and at herp expos. They are highly aggressive and nervous, and do not do well in small or crowded quarters. They need a large, tall cage with plenty of climbing surfaces. They generally cannot be kept with any smaller species, but in a very large enclosure, you could try mixing them with other tropical forest lizards, such as basilisks or monkey-tailed skinks. Given their large size, knight

Several subspecies of the Martinique anole, A. roquet, *are bred by European hobbyists and trickle into the US hobby. Keep them like green anoles but slightly warmer.*

Other Anoles   61

Mixing Species

Given their small size and easy care, green anoles and some of the other species lend themselves well to naturalistic enclosures with a mix of other herps. In a large enclosure, this is a possibility that makes for a fascinating and impressive display. However, you do have to exercise some care in mixing various species. Mixing species can be dangerous for the creatures, as not all animals get along. If you decide to mix in some other animals, there are a few guidelines to follow. First, all of the animals have to have similar care requirements. Second, all should be of similar size to prevent them from eating each other or out-competing each other for food. Third, the keeper must be prepared to give the different species their own cage should the mixing not work out.

The following is a list of some species that should do well in a terrarium with a small anole species or two. There may be others that will work, also. You should research each species' requirements before you decide to add it to your anole habitat.

Fire-bellied Toad, *Bombina orientalis* (requires a swimming area)

Flying Gecko, various species of *Ptychozoon*

Gold Dust Day Gecko, *Phelsuma laticauda* (other small day geckos are possibilities)

Gray Treefrog, *Hyla chrysoscelis* and *Hyla versicolor*

Green Treefrog, *Hyla cinerea*

anoles are capable of eating much larger prey than typical *Anolis*. You can try offering them king mealworms, large silkworms, various species of giant roaches, smaller lizards, and mice.

This anole is sometimes captive bred. The captive-bred babies become rather tame if they are handled consistently and gently. However, be aware that adult knight anoles pack a bad bite.

Resources

MAGAZINES

Reptiles Magazine
P.O. Box 6050
Mission Viejo, CA 92690
www.animalnetwork.com/reptiles

Contemporary Herpetology
Southeastern Louisiana University
www.nhm.ac.uk/hosted_sites/ch

Herp Digest
www.herpdigest.org

ORGANIZATIONS

*American Society of Ichthyologists and
Herpetologists*
Maureen Donnelly, Secretary
Grice Marine Laboratory
Florida International University
Biological Sciences
11200 SW 8th St.
Miami, FL 33199
Telephone: (305) 348-1235
E-mail: asih@fiu.edu
www.asih.org

Amphibian, Reptile & Insect Association
Liz Price
23 Windmill Rd
Irthlingsborough
Wellingborough NN9 5RJ
England

British Herpetological Society
Zoological Society of London
Regent Park
London NW1 4RY
www.thebhs.org

*Society for the Study of Amphibians and
Reptiles (SSAR)*
Marion Preest, Secretary
The Claremont Colleges
925 N. Mills Ave.
Claremont, CA 91711
Phone: 909-607-8014
E-mail: mpreest@jsd.claremont.edu
www.ssarherps.org

WEB RESOURCES

Anole Forest
www.geocities.com/dozergh91/index.html

Anolis Contact Group
www.come.to/anoliscontactgroup

Caribbean Anole Database
www.homestead.com/Anolis/

EMBL Reptile Database
www.reptiliaweb.org

HerpNetwork
www.herpnetwork.com

Herp Societies and Rescues
www.anapsid.org/societies

Kingsnake
www.kingsnake.com

Kingsnake (UK)
www.kingsnake.co.uk

List of US Herp Societies
www.kingsnake.com/society.html

*The Societas Europea Herp (European Herp
Society)*
www.gli.cas.cz/seh

VETERINARY RESOURCES

*Association of Reptile and Amphibian
Veterinarians*
P.O. Box 605
Chester Heights, PA 19017
Phone: 610-358-9530
Fax: 610-892-4813
E-mail: ARAVETS@aol.com
www.arav.org

Herp Vet Connection (US & International)
www.herpvetconnection.com

RESCUE AND ADOPTION SERVICES

ASPCA
424 East 92nd Street
New York, NY 10128-6801
Phone: (212) 876-7700
E-mail: information@aspca.org
www.aspca.org

RSPCA (UK)
Wilberforce Way
Southwater
Horsham, West Sussex RH13 9RS
Telephone: 0870 3335 999
www.rspca.org.uk

Index

Measurement Conversion Chart

UNITS USED IN THIS BOOK
1 gallon = 3.7854 liters
1 inch = 2.54 centimeters
32°F = 0°C (water freezes)
75°F = 23.9°C

CONVERTING FAHRENHEIT TO CELSIUS
Subtract 32 from the Fahrenheit temperature.
Divide the answer by 9.
Multiply that answer by 5.

Photo Credits

R. D. Bartlett: 6, 13, 26, 30, 31, 34, 53, 60, 61 (top)
Allen R. Both: 54
Suzanne L. Collins: 24, 55, 56 (bottom)
I. Francais: 18, 48
M. Gilroy: 3, 5, 7, 9, 12, 16, 25, 32, 39, 47 (bottom), 49
V. T. Jirousek: 59
Barry Mansell: 58 (bottom)
Sean McKeown: 14, 17
G. & C. Merker: 4
A. Norman: 1
M. Panzella: 45
E. Radford: 40
Mark Smith: 21, 52, 61 (bottom)
R. G. Sprackland: 51
K. H. Switak: 15, 47 (top)
TFH Archives: 56 (top), 58 (top)
John Tyson: 41
J. G. & M. Walls: 23
R. T. Zappalorti: 27

Quick and Easy Green Anole Care